Please return items on or before the
on your receipt.
**Register your email address and you will receive a
reminder before your books are due back.**
You can register your email address, check the Due
Date and renew your loans online at
www.dublincitypubliclibraries.ie
Have your Library Card Number and PIN to hand.
You can also renew your loans in person or by phone.

**Leabharlanna Poiblí Chathair Bhaile Átha Cliath
Dublin City Public Libraries**

 Comhairle Cathrach
Bhaile Átha Cliath
Dublin City Council

BRIAN McDERMOTT is Chef Patron of the award-winning boutique Foyle Hotel. An award-winning chef who is passionate about sharing his love of food with others, Brian is the author of the successful cookery books *Brian McDermott's Donegal Table* and *Reunite with Food* and is a regular on RTÉ and BBC television and radio, and in the local and national press. He lives in Moville with his wife, Brenda, and daughters, Niamh and Aoife.

CONTENTS

First published 2019 by
The O'Brien Press Ltd,
12 Terenure Road East, Rathgar, Dublin 6, D06 HD27, Ireland.
Tel: +353 1 4923333; Fax: +353 1 4922777
E-mail: books@obrien.ie; Website: www.obrien.ie
The O'Brien Press is a member of Publishing Ireland.

ISBN: 978-1-78849-047-4

Photography by A Fox in the Kitchen.
Photographs on pages 6 & 70 courtesy of Carsten Krieger.

6 5 4 3 2 1
21 20 19

Printed and bound in Drukarnia Skleniarz, Poland.
The paper in this book is produced using pulp from managed forests.

Published in:

DUBLIN
UNESCO
City of Literature

INTRODUCTION

As one of twelve children growing up in County Donegal in Ireland, my mother's kitchen table was the focal point of the family. She was always there, cooking and baking, usually with one or two of us at her feet looking for a slice of soda bread or a piece of cake. When all twelve of us were around it could get pretty crowded, but even from a young age I loved the sense of belonging I felt in that kitchen – me and my parents and my brothers and sisters, all sitting down to eat together. I loved the craic, too – many's the story that was told around that table, especially when relatives or neighbours called in!

I didn't realise it at the time, of course, but it was some achievement keeping us all fed and happy in the days before microwaves, ready-meals and takeaways. We ate what my father would have called 'good, honest food'. There was always a pot of stew on the go and plenty of spuds. It was only later that I realised that practically everything we ate was local. Our meat and vegetables came from local farms, and our fish came straight from the pier and could be in the pan within the hour. My dad could have told you the field our dinner came from or the fisherman who had caught it.

Looking back, I realise that my own journey with food started at that kitchen table. My mother will tell you I always loved to eat, but I always loved to cook too. I've always believed that tasty, healthy food based around traditional Irish recipes and local produce is something everyone can make and enjoy; these recipes sum up the best of what Ireland has to offer. It's what inspires me every day – and I hope it will inspire you too.

Brian McDermott

Breakfast
&
Brunch

Crispy Mackerel on Toast

The lime juice and rocket pesto really brings out that summery feel of fresh-caught Irish mackerel.

SERVES 4

FOR THE PESTO

Good handful of rocket

3 tbsp rapeseed oil

2 cloves of garlic

2 tbsp red wine vinegar

Freshly ground black pepper

50 g blue cheese (or cheese of your choice)

4 tsp sesame seeds

FOR THE MACKEREL

1 tsp chilli powder

Freshly ground black pepper

50 g plain flour

4 slices ciabatta bread

200 ml rapeseed oil

4 mackerel fillets

60 g crème fraiche

1 lime, cut into 4 wedges

1. To make the pesto, put all the ingredients except the sesame seeds in a blender and combine until you have a smooth-ish paste. Toast the sesame seeds on a flat, dry pan until golden brown, making sure you stay at the pan and toss them continuously. Add them to the blended pesto.

2. For the mackerel, first combine the chilli powder and black pepper with the flour.

3. Toast the slices of ciabatta bread and drizzle with some of the rapeseed oil, then set aside.

4. Heat a wok and add the rest of the rapeseed oil. Pat both sides of the mackerel fillets in the flour then place in the hot oil. Cook each fillet for about 2 minutes on each side, until crispy.

5. Spoon some crème fraiche onto each slice of ciabatta and place a piece of mackerel on top. Drizzle with rocket pesto and a squeeze of lime.

Tip

Pesto will keep for three weeks in a sealed container in the fridge.

It tastes great with pork, chicken, salads and pasta.

Bacon on Eggy Bread with Field Mushrooms

Eggy bread is one of life's pleasures when done right. Top it with crispy bacon and mushrooms and it's perfect for any occasion.

SERVES 4

8 rashers dry-cured streaky bacon
4 eggs
50 ml milk
Pinch of cinnamon
Freshly ground black pepper
4 slices of bread
Drizzle of rapeseed oil

50 g butter
8 mushrooms, sliced
Sprig of fresh thyme
Handful of rocket leaves
40 g tomato ketchup

1. Heat the grill and grill the bacon until crispy.
2. Whisk the eggs in a bowl with the milk, cinnamon and a twist of black pepper.
3. Place the bread in the egg mix for one minute to soak.
4. Heat a large frying pan and add a drizzle of oil and half of the butter. Add the slices of bread and cook on medium heat until golden brown on both sides.
5. Place the bread in a warm oven, and in the same pan add the rest of the butter and fry the sliced mushrooms with the sprig of thyme and some more black pepper.
6. Serve the bread with the rocket, bacon, mushrooms and a dollop of ketchup.

Tip

This is also great with quality sausages from your local butcher.

Omelette

Omelettes work with almost any ingredients. I've chosen bacon, tomatoes and basil for this recipe, but they are so versatile that you can experiment with virtually anything.

SERVES 1

2 slices dry-cured bacon

3 eggs

Freshly ground black pepper

Knob of butter

1 tomato, chopped

30 g Cheddar cheese, grated

Handful of fresh basil

1. Warm your grill to a medium heat.

2. Place the bacon slices on a tray and grill for 5 minutes, turning halfway through.

3. Crack the eggs into a bowl and season with pepper. Using a fork, whisk the eggs until they're light and bubbly.

4. Heat a non-stick omelette pan over a medium heat and melt a knob of butter. Add the beaten eggs to the pan and stir using a spatula, then allow the eggs to settle in the pan and cook for 1 minute.

5. Add the chopped tomatoes and cooked bacon slices on top of the omelette and sprinkle the cheese over. Place the pan under the grill for 2 minutes. The omelette will puff up slightly.

6. Loosen it from the pan and fold it over onto itself. Serve with fresh basil scattered on top.

Tip:

If you have a few people to feed, treble the recipe and make it in a larger pan. Slice your omelette like a breakfast pizza.

Soups
&
Snacks

Big, Hearty Veggie Broth

This nutritional powerhouse of a soup tastes even better on the second day as all the ingredients concentrate as the soup reduces in volume to create that big, hearty veggie broth flavour.

SERVES 4

100 g barley

50 g butter

3 cloves of garlic, crushed

1 onion, peeled and diced

150 g leeks, washed and sliced

150 g carrots, peeled and diced

150 g celery, washed and diced

2 bay leaves

200 g potatoes, peeled and diced

Freshly ground white pepper

2 litres vegetable stock

Handful of chopped fresh parsley

1. Soak the barley in cold water for at least 20 minutes.

2. Melt the butter in a saucepan and sweat the crushed garlic, onion, leeks, carrots and celery with the bay leaves for 5 minutes. Add the potatoes and soaked barley.

3. Season with pepper and cover with the vegetable stock.

4. Bring to the boil and allow to simmer for 20 minutes or until the barley is cooked.

5. Add the parsley and serve piping hot.

Tip

Replace the vegetable stock with homemade chicken stock, made using a whole chicken. Remove the meat from the carcass and add it to the soup pot to turn your veggie broth into a hearty chicken soup.

Turnip, Leek and Potato Soup

Turnips are very popular in Ireland, they have a wonderful flavour and, when used properly in a soup, really turn it into something special.

SERVES 4–6
50 g butter
200 g small onions, chopped
4 cloves of garlic, crushed
200 g leeks, trimmed and chopped
200 g celery sticks, trimmed and chopped

200 g turnips, peeled and diced
200 g potatoes, peeled and diced
2 litres hot vegetable stock
Sprig of tarragon, chopped
Freshly ground black pepper
150 ml cream

1. Melt the butter in a large saucepan and sweat the onions and garlic in it for a few minutes. Then add the leeks, celery, turnips and potatoes.
2. Sweat for a further 4–5 minutes, stirring all the time, and then add the stock, tarragon and pepper.
3. Simmer for about 15 minutes, until the vegetables are soft, then add the cream and remove from the heat.
4. Blend the soup in a blender and serve piping hot.

Tip

Try replacing turnip with celeriac for an earthier flavour and creamier texture.

Black Pudding Dipping Fritters

Black pudding is a nutritional 'superfood' according to many sources, and it's been a favourite in Ireland for generations. Using pudding to create these tasty dippers is a little different and makes a great starter.

SERVES 4–6
FOR THE FILLING
300 g black pudding
1 apple, peeled and grated
40 g butter
6 leaves of fresh sage

FOR THE CRUMB
200 g breadcrumbs
100 g porridge oats
50 g flour
3 eggs, beaten

1 LITRE VEGETABLE OIL, FOR FRYING
Apple chutney, to serve

1. Preheat the oven to 170°C/325°F/Gas Mark 3.
2. To make the black pudding filling, simply place all the ingredients in a blender and blend until combined. Then shape into round, bite-size shapes.
3. Next, mix the breadcrumbs and porridge oats together. Roll each dipper in the flour and then the beaten egg. Then finely coat them in the breadcrumb and porridge-oat mix.

4. Heat the oil in a deep fat fryer or deep pot to 170°C/325°F. Fry the puddings until golden in colour. Place on a tray and cook in the oven for 5 minutes.
5. Serve with some apple chutney for dipping.

Goats' Cheese Tartlets

Goat's cheese is sweet and when heated with red onion chutney it tastes mild and delicious. I've suggested making these as individual tartlets, but this recipe will work just as well as a large 25 cm tart.

SERVES 12

4 red onions, thinly sliced

Drizzle of rapeseed oil

150 g dark brown sugar

60 ml balsamic vinegar

60 ml red wine

1 packet puff pastry

150 g good quality roasted red peppers from a jar, sliced

120 g soft goat's cheese

120 ml cream

Few sprigs of thyme

1. Preheat the oven to 190°C/375°F/Gas Mark 5. Grease a 12-cup muffin tray.

2. Fry the red onions in a drizzle of oil for 4–5 minutes. Then add the sugar to caramelise them. Cook on a low heat for a further 5 minutes until slightly sticky.

3. Add the balsamic vinegar and red wine and allow to simmer for 15 minutes.

4. Roll out 400 g of the puff pastry. Cut out 12 large discs with a biscuit cutter and use them to line each greased cup of the muffin tin.

5. Place a piece of roasted red pepper in the base of each cup with some of the onion mix. Add the goat's cheese on top. Pour in a dollop of cream and top with a sprig of fresh thyme leaves.

6. Place in the oven and bake for 30 minutes or until the pastry is golden.

Tip

Add some pesto on top of the cheese for an even tastier version.

The Ultimate Open Farm Sandwich

Any sandwich is made instantly better with a homemade ploughman's pickle. This pickle recipe is easy to make and keeps for months in the fridge. Leftover cooked beef from a Sunday roast is perfect for this sandwich.

FOR THE PLOUGHMAN'S PICKLE

1 onion, diced
1 courgette, diced
150 g carrots, peeled and diced
150 g turnip, peeled and diced
4 cloves of garlic, crushed
1 cucumber, diced
Juice of 1 lemon
200 ml malt vinegar
175 g brown sugar
1 tbsp ground allspice

FOR THE SANDWICH

1 onion, sliced
Drizzle of rapeseed oil
Freshly ground black pepper
4 slices of ciabatta
1 iceberg lettuce
400 g cooked leftover beef
8 slices of tomato
4 slices of mature Cheddar

1. To make the pickle, place all the ingredients in a pot and simmer until the turnips are cooked and the pickle is almost sticky. If the consistency becomes too thick, add a drop of boiling water to loosen it. When cooked and cooled, place in sterilised jars with a lid and seal.

2. For the sandwich, first fry the onion in the oil and season with pepper.

3. Heat the bread in the oven or under the grill. Place a few leaves of lettuce on each piece of warm bread and arrange thin slices of the leftover beef on top. Next, arrange the tomato slices and spread with the warm onions and then the slices of cheese.

4. Top with the pickle.

Tip

Add a layer of mustard or mayonnaise to the warm bread for added flavour.

Fishy-fishy

Middle-of-the-Table Mussels with Dry-Cured Bacon

I always serve my mussels in the middle of the table in the pot they were cooked in. It looks and smells great, and there's no better way to encourage my guests to get stuck in!

SERVES 6

4 rashers dry-cured bacon

2 kg Irish mussels

3 cloves of garlic, crushed

1 bay leaf

1 small onion, diced

50 ml white wine

150 ml cream

Freshly ground black pepper

Handful of fresh parsley, chopped

Crusty bread (for dipping)

1. Grill the rashers of bacon until crispy, then set aside. Wait until they've cooled, then cut them into strips.

2. Wash the mussels in cold water. Discard any open mussels.

3. Place the mussels, garlic, bay leaf, onion and white wine into a large pot, and cover with a lid. Place on the hob for about 6 minutes, shaking the pot a couple of times during cooking. The mussels should all have opened – remove any that remain closed.

4. Add the cream, pepper and chopped parsley and cook for a further 2 minutes. Remove from the heat and add the strips of bacon.

5. Serve with crusty bread to soak up the scrumptious sauce.

Pan-Fried Hake with Rosemary, Leeks and Poached Egg

If you want more fish in your diet then hake is an excellent choice, as it's easy to cook, soft in texture and has far fewer bones than any other fish.

SERVES 4

Drizzle of rapeseed oil
40 g butter
600 g fresh hake fillets
2 sprigs of rosemary
Freshly ground black pepper

1 lemon
½ leek, sliced
½ onion, sliced
1 clove of garlic, crushed
100 ml cream
4 free-range eggs

1. Heat a frying pan and add a drizzle of rapeseed oil and half the butter. Place the hake in the pan, skin-side down, and cook for 2 minutes. Add the sprigs of rosemary.
2. Turn the hake over, season with black pepper and add the zest of the lemon. Cook on medium heat for 4 minutes, then transfer the fish to a warm tray.
3. Using the same pan, add the rest of the butter, followed by the leek, onion and garlic. Reduce the heat and sweat for 2–3 minutes.

Add the cream and allow it to warm through. Season with freshly ground black pepper.
4. While the leeks are sweating, heat some water in a saucepan until light bubbles appear, as in a glass of lemonade. Crack and gently drop the eggs into the water and cook for about 2 minutes, ensuring you retain a soft runny egg.
5. Serve the hake on top of the vegetables and place the poached egg on top. Sprinkle with some more pepper.

Tip

Try replacing the hake with cod, haddock or turbot.

Wild Atlantic Way Fish Pie

The Wild Atlantic Way is one of the longest coastal routes in Europe, so it's only fitting to include a dish that celebrates the freshness of the sea.

SERVES 6

100 g butter

Bunch of scallions, finely chopped

Freshly ground black pepper

750 g potatoes, cooked and mashed

350 g haddock fillets

350 g smoked haddock fillets

1 bay leaf

500 ml milk

50 g plain flour

100 g local cheese, grated

1 onion, peeled and diced

2 carrots, peeled and diced

White of 1 leek, sliced

4 sticks of celery, diced

50 ml rapeseed oil

4 cloves of garlic, crushed

Handful of fresh parsley, chopped

1. Melt 50 g of the butter in a pan and sweat the chopped scallions. Mix in through the mashed potato along with a pinch of pepper. Leave aside.

2. Preheat the oven to 200°C/400°F/ Gas Mark 6.

3. Place the fish fillets in a pan with the bay leaf and cover with the milk. Bring to the boil and simmer for 7 minutes.

4. Remove the fish from the milk and place in tin foil to keep warm.

5. Melt the remainder of the butter in a saucepan and add the flour to make a roux. Cook for 1 minute. Gradually add the milk the fish was cooked in, and season with pinch of pepper. Stirring all the time, simmer the sauce until it thickens. Add 50 g of the grated cheese.

6. Sweat the garlic, onion, carrots, leek and celery in the rapeseed oil until the vegetables have softened.

7. Roughly break up the fish fillets, then place in an ovenproof dish with the vegetables. Pour over the sauce and gently combine. Spread the mashed potato on top and sprinkle with the remaining grated cheese. Bake in the preheated oven for 40 minutes.

8. Allow to rest for 10 minutes before serving. Garnish with chopped parsley.

Fish Stew

A fish stew is basically a heartier version of chowder. I like to create a really wholesome, creamy texture for my stews by poaching the fish in milk. This captures all the delicious taste of the fish and makes a perfect stock for your stew.

SERVES 6

200 g salmon, boned and skinned
200 g smoked whiting or haddock, boned and skinned
200 g unsmoked haddock, boned and skinned
500 ml milk
2 bay leaves
50 g butter
1 onion, diced
2 cloves of garlic, crushed
2 sticks of celery, peeled and diced

Half a leek, thinly sliced
2 carrots, peeled and diced
Half a bulb of fennel, diced
3 sprigs of thyme
50 g plain flour
Sprinkle of dried dill
2 potatoes, peeled and diced
Freshly ground black pepper
Drop of Worcestershire sauce
Fresh chives or parsley, chopped, to serve

1. Place the boned and skinless fish in a pot and add the milk and 1 bay leaf. Bring to the boil, then reduce the heat and poach for 8 minutes.

2. In a separate pot, melt the butter and sweat the diced onion, crushed garlic, celery, leek, carrots, fennel, remaining bay leaf and sprigs of thyme for 3–4 minutes.

3. Add the flour and mix in thoroughly. Then add the dill.

4. Drain the milk from the fish and add the milk straight in with the vegetables. Add the diced potatoes and stir occasionally.

5. Season with the freshly ground pepper and a drop of Worcestershire sauce and cook for 15 minutes on a low heat, stirring occasionally. The stew will thicken.

6. Add some broken fish pieces to a bowl and serve the stew over them, piping hot.

7. Serve with a sprinkle of fresh chives or parsley

Tip

This is great with some homemade brown bread.

Hearty Irish Dinners

Cabbage and Bacon with Parsley Sauce

This is a very traditional Irish dish; when made with Irish bacon and fresh cabbage, the flavours are amazing.

SERVES 4

700 g back bacon
1 onion, finely chopped
6 cloves
1 head green savoy cabbage, shredded
Freshly ground black pepper

60 g butter
60 g plain flour
100 ml white wine
150 ml cream
200 ml reserved cooking liquid
Handful of parsley, chopped

1. Place the bacon in the pot with the onion and cloves and cover with cold water.
2. Bring to the boil and simmer gently for 1 hour. Save the cooking liquid for the sauce.
3. Cook the cabbage in boiling water for 12–14 minutes. Drain, season with pepper and set aside.
4. Meanwhile, melt the butter in a saucepan and add the flour. Stir until you have a paste, and cook for 2 minutes.

5. Mix the wine, cream and 200 ml of the cooking liquid from the bacon together. Add slowly to the flour and butter, stirring all the time – the sauce will thicken gradually. Add the chopped parsley to the sauce and leave aside in a warm place.
6. Slice the bacon while warm and serve with the cabbage and a generous amount of the parsley sauce.

Tip

This is delicious with boiled new potatoes.

Beef and Ale Casserole

The ale adds a real bitter flavour to this dish, and it's a perfect winter warmer for the cold nights in. Ask your butcher for a shin of beef to use in this recipe.

SERVES 6

Drizzle of rapeseed oil

1 kg beef shin, cubed

2 onions, diced

4 cloves of garlic, crushed

2 bay leaves

2 carrots, peeled and diced

2 sticks of celery, sliced

25 g tomato puree

25 g plain flour

250 ml local ale

220 ml beef stock

2 sprigs of fresh thyme

Freshly ground black pepper

8 mushrooms, sliced

1. Preheat the oven to 170°C/325°F/Gas Mark 3.

2. Add a drizzle of oil to a casserole pot and brown half of the meat pieces. Remove, then brown the second half.

3. Return all the beef to the pot and add the onions, garlic, bay leaves, carrots and celery and cook for 5 minutes, stirring occasionally.

4. Add the tomato puree and flour and mix well. Then add the ale and stir it through the vegetables and beef. Top it up by adding the beef stock and the sprigs of thyme, and then season with pepper.

5. Add the sliced mushrooms and simmer for 10 minutes. Put on the lid and transfer to the oven for 3 hours, stirring every 30 minutes.

Mammy's Irish Stew

I don't think there is a person in Ireland who hasn't enjoyed an Irish mammy's Irish stew at some point in their lives; it's the taste of home.

SERVES 6

1 kg diced Irish lamb (preferably shoulder cut)
2 bay leaves
Drizzle of rapeseed oil
2 cloves of garlic, crushed
1 onion, peeled and diced
1 carrot, peeled and diced
½ leek, diced
1 parsnip, peeled and diced
2 sprigs of fresh thyme
Freshly ground black pepper
4 potatoes, peeled and diced
2 litres warm chicken stock
Handful of young cabbage leaves, chopped

1. Cover the lamb pieces in water and simmer with one of the bay leaves for about 20 minutes.
2. Heat a casserole pot, add the oil and sweat the vegetables, starting with the garlic and onion and followed by the carrot, leek and parsnip.
3. Add the sprigs of thyme and the remaining bay leaf. Season with black pepper. Sweat for roughly 5 minutes, stirring all the time, then add the diced potato.
4. Drain the lamb and immediately add the meat to the vegetables. Cover with the warm stock. Put on the lid and simmer for about 1 hour, stirring occasionally.
5. After an hour, add the chopped cabbage and check if the lamb is tender. If not, cook for a further 20 minutes.
6. Serve this hearty dish in a bowl and enjoy with family and friends.

Tip

Scoop out the inside of a round sourdough bap, leaving just the crust, and serve the stew inside the bread.

Sunday's Finest Roast Lemon and Thyme Chicken

A roast chicken on a Sunday is simply scrumptious, and the leftovers picked from the bones are just as tasty that evening or the next day. Chicken can be fairly bland but lemon and thyme pack a big punch, which is why they work so well in this recipe.

SERVES 4

1 kg whole chicken
Drizzle of rapeseed oil
Freshly ground black pepper
6 sprigs of fresh thyme

1 lemon
6 cloves of garlic
1 onion
2 carrots
100 ml cider or apple juice

1. Preheat the oven to 190°C/375°F/Gas Mark 5.

2. Brush the skin of the chicken with oil. Season with black pepper and sprinkle with fresh thyme.

3. Zest the lemon and rub the zest around the breasts and legs of the chicken. Cut the zested lemon into slices and place underneath the chicken. Place the garlic cloves inside.

4. Peel the onion and carrots, then slice in half and place in a roasting tray. Set the chicken on top. Add the cider or apple juice to the base of the tray and place in the oven.

5. Roast the chicken for 1 hour. Allow to rest for about 20 minutes, and then slice and serve with the juices from the tray drizzled over the meat.

Tip

Leftover chicken is great in wraps, salads or sandwiches. Roast two chickens and keep one to start the week with great packed lunches or easy dinners at home.

Irish Cottage Pie

Cottage pie is the ultimate comfort food. It's simple – a meat base with gravy and a thick layer of mashed potatoes – and it's the sort of dish that's been served in family homes in Ireland for generations. There's a reason why it's still eaten – and adored – by young and old!

SERVES 4–6

Drizzle of rapeseed oil
500 g minced beef
1 onion, peeled and chopped
2 carrots, peeled and diced
3 cloves of garlic, crushed
150 g mushrooms, sliced
1 bay leaf
40 g plain flour
400 g tinned chopped tomatoes
50 g tomato puree
1 litre beef stock
Drop of Worcestershire sauce
450 g mashed potato
Knob of butter, melted
Freshly ground black pepper

1. Preheat the oven to 180°C/350°F/Gas Mark 3
2. In a saucepan, heat the rapeseed oil and brown the minced beef, stirring all the time to break up the meat. Add the onion, carrots and garlic, followed by the mushrooms. Then drop in the bay leaf and lightly fry for a further 4–5 minutes.
3. Add the flour and mix thoroughly. Then add the chopped tomatoes and tomato puree, followed by the stock.
4. Allow to simmer for 25 minutes, stirring occasionally. Remove from the heat and season with pepper and a drop of Worcestershire sauce.
5. Heat the mashed potato.
6. Spoon the cottage-pie filling into an earthenware dish and spread a layer of mashed potato on top. Brush with the melted butter, sprinkle with some black pepper and place in the oven for 15 minutes.
7. Serve in warmed bowls.

Lamb and Barley Hot Pot

This dish is so simple to make, but it's always a real winner. It's healthy and nutritious, but it also has that one-pot comfort-food vibe which never goes wrong, especially in the winter.

SERVES 6

75 g barley
1 tbsp rapeseed oil
600 g lamb, diced
3 cloves of garlic, sliced
2 small onions, diced
2 bay leaves
3 sprigs of fresh thyme

Freshly ground black pepper
1 carrot, diced
1 parsnip, diced
2 sticks of celery, thinly sliced
1 litre vegetable stock, warmed
4 medium potatoes
Handful of fresh parsley

1. Preheat the oven to 170°C/325°F/Gas Mark 3.

2. Cook the barley in boiling water for approximately 25 minutes. Drain and leave aside.

3. Heat a casserole dish, add some of the oil and lightly colour the diced lamb. Add the garlic, onions, bay leaves and 2 sprigs of thyme, and sweat for a few minutes.

4. Season with pepper, then add the carrot, parsnip and celery and continue to cook for a further 5 minutes.

5. Add the cooked barley followed by the warmed stock. Cover with a lid and simmer for approximately 40 minutes or until the lamb is tender.

6. While the lamb is cooking, peel and thinly slice the potatoes. Pan fry them in the rest of the oil, turning regularly, until tender. Remove the leaves from the remaining sprig of thyme and sprinkle over the potatoes. Season with pepper.

7. Arrange the potatoes on top of the lamb and replace in the oven for a further 15 minutes.

Veggie Summer Tart

This dish doesn't even need one pot, just one 25 cm flan tin. I think of it as a challenge to see how many vegetables I can pack in! I've included a recipe to make your own pastry for this. It's very easy to make pastry at home and, as you'll find out, it's well worth the effort!

SERVES 8

FOR THE PASTRY

250 g plain flour

125 g butter, softened, plus a little extra for greasing

1 egg

35 ml water

FOR THE FILLING

Drizzle of rapeseed oil

1 red onion, sliced

2 cloves of garlic, sliced

½ red pepper, diced

2 sprigs of thyme

Freshly ground black pepper

8 sprigs of early sprouting broccoli

Handful of cabbage leaves, chopped

10 cherry tomatoes, halved

90 g cheese of your choice, grated

2 eggs

100 ml cream

1. Preheat the oven to 180°C/350°F/Gas Mark 4.

2 To make the pastry, rub the butter into the flour until it has a sandy, breadcrumb texture. Add the egg and the water and combine to form a firm pastry. Wrap in cling film and allow to rest in the fridge for 20 minutes.

3. Use a little melted butter to grease a 25 cm flan tin.

4. Roll out the pastry and line the tin with it. Place a disc of greaseproof paper on top of the pastry and fill with baking beans.

5. Blind bake the pastry case for 15 minutes.

6. While the pastry is baking, heat a frying pan, add a drizzle of oil and fry the onion, garlic and pepper with sprigs of fresh thyme. Season with black pepper.

7. Boil some water and cook the broccoli and

cabbage in it for 2 minutes, then place in cold water to ensure they stay green.

8. When the pastry is cooked, remove the greaseproof paper and beans and allow it to cool.

9. When the pastry is cool, place half of the cooked vegetables and half of the cherry tomatoes into the pastry case and sprinkle with 1/3 of the grated cheese, then fill up with the remaining vegetables and another 1/3 of the cheese.

Whisk the eggs and cream together, season with black pepper and pour into the pastry case on top of the vegetables. Sprinkle with the remaining cheese and bake for 30 minutes.

Orzo Pasta with Bacon and Cabbage

Orzo pasta is so easy to cook that you can make this tasty dish in fifteen minutes.

SERVES 4

300 g orzo pasta

6 rashers dry-cured bacon

Rapeseed oil

4 cloves of garlic, sliced

2 sprigs of fresh thyme

Freshly ground black pepper

3 leaves cabbage/kale

40 g butter

80 ml cream

80 g Parmesan cheese, grated

TO SERVE

10 g Parmesan cheese, grated

Handful of fresh basil

1. Add the orzo pasta to a pot of boiling water and cook for 8 minutes.

2. While the pasta is cooking, slice the bacon into strips.

3. Heat a drizzle of rapeseed oil in a frying pan then add the garlic followed by the bacon. Cook for a few minutes then drop in the thyme and a sprinkle of black pepper.

4. Roll the washed cabbage or kale leaves and shred. Add to the pan and cook for 2 minutes, then add the butter and cream and simmer for 3 minutes.

5. Drain the pasta and add another drizzle of rapeseed oil. Combine the pasta with the bacon and cabbage or kale in the pot. Add the grated Parmesan and lightly stir.

6. Serve in pasta bowls with more Parmesan and some basil leaves sprinkled on top.

Tip

For a slightly spicier dish, replace the bacon with chorizo or try adding some diced red peppers and chopped basil.

Herby Roast Leg of Lamb

Irish lamb is among the best in the world, and this dish is a real favourite.

SERVES 4

4 cloves of garlic, peeled

5 sprigs of thyme

6 mint leaves

2 sprigs of rosemary

Freshly ground black pepper

Drizzle of rapeseed oil

Zest of 1 lemon

1 leg of lamb (roughly 2kg)

2 potatoes, peeled and cut into quarters

2 onions, halved

2 carrots, peeled and halved

Splash of red wine

100 ml hot chicken stock

1 tbsp tomato puree

1. Preheat the oven to 170°C/325°F/Gas Mark 3.

2. Using a pestle and mortar, crush the peeled garlic with the thyme, mint, rosemary and black pepper. Add a drizzle of oil and the lemon zest.

3. Rub the mixture over the whole surface of the lamb.

4. Place the potatoes, onions and carrots in a roasting dish and rest the lamb on top of the vegetables.

5. Cover the lamb with tin foil. Roast in the oven for two hours, or until cooked to your liking.

6. When cooked, remove the lamb and set on a tray to rest for at least 15 minutes before carving.

7. While the meat is resting, place the roasting dish on the hob over a medium heat and add a splash of red wine and then the hot stock. Stir with a wooden spoon, scraping up anything that's stuck to the tray, and mash the vegetables to thicken the gravy.

8. Add 250 ml of boiling water and the tomato puree and allow to simmer for 10 minutes. Strain and pour your gravy over the freshly carved lamb.

Potatoes, Spuds, Praties ...

Perfect Mash

Rule number one for perfect mash – it must have cream, milk and butter. The next step is to make sure the potatoes are properly cooked – that means until they're soft – and then drained fully to remove excess water. Returning the drained potatoes to the stove for a minute will further dry out the potatoes prior to mashing and help ensure you get perfect mash, every time.

SERVES 4

1 kg potatoes
100 ml milk
75 ml cream
50 g butter
Freshly ground white pepper
Pinch of nutmeg

1. Wash and peel the potatoes, and then cook in boiling water until soft. Drain off the cooking water and return the potatoes to the heat for a minute to allow any remaining moisture to evaporate.

2. In a separate saucepan heat the milk, cream and butter until the butter has melted.

3. Season the potatoes with ground white pepper and nutmeg, then mash.

4. When the potatoes are mashed, add the liquid and return the potatoes to the heat. Keep mashing constantly until you have no lumps.

5. You should now have perfect mash.

Tip

Add some grated cheese for cheesy mash.

Poundies versus Champ

In some parts of Ireland they're called 'poundies', in others 'champ', but they're delicious whatever they're called.

SERVES 4
1 kg potatoes, peeled
50 g butter
6 scallions, sliced

100 ml milk
75 ml cream
Freshly ground white pepper
Pinch of nutmeg

1. Wash and peel the potatoes, then cook in boiling water until soft. Drain off the cooking water and return the potatoes to the heat for a minute to allow any remaining moisture to evaporate.

2. In a separate saucepan, melt the butter with the scallions until the mixture sweats. Cook for 2 minutes, then add the milk and cream and allow the liquid to warm.

3. Season the potatoes with ground white pepper and nutmeg, then mash. When all the potatoes are mashed, add the liquid and return the potatoes to the heat. Keep mashing constantly until you have no lumps.

Tip

Turn any leftover poundies into potato cakes by shaping them into rounds and pan-frying them in butter.

Colcannon

This dish is so good it's almost a meal in itself.

SERVES 4

1 kg potatoes
100 g butter
250 g curly kale, finely sliced

Freshly ground black pepper
100 ml milk, warmed

1. Cook the potatoes in boiling water for 15 minutes or until tender.
2. To cook the kale, heat a knob of the butter in a saucepan and cook the kale in it for 2 minutes. Season with pepper.
3. Drain the potatoes, add in the milk and mash until smooth. Then beat in the kale and the remaining butter.

Tip

If young kale leaves are not available, use cabbage leaves. Simply cook the cabbage first by boiling it, and then proceed as above.

Coddle

While coddle is associated with Dublin, it's eaten all over the country.

SERVES 8

Drizzle of rapeseed oil

450 g sausages

200 g bacon, cut into strips

1 onion, diced

2 carrots, sliced

1 kg potatoes, peeled and sliced

Freshly ground black pepper

500 ml chicken stock, warmed

1 bay leaf

Handful of fresh parsley, chopped

1. Preheat the oven to 170°C/325°F/Gas Mark 3.
2. Heat the oil in a frying pan and brown the sausages. Add the bacon and cook for 2 minutes.
3. Place half of the bacon and sausages in the bottom of an earthenware dish and add half the onions, carrots and potatoes.
4. Season with pepper, and repeat with another layer of meat and vegetables. Pour the warm stock over and add the bay leaf.
5. Cover with a lid and cook for 2 hours. Remove the lid and cook for a further 30 minutes.
6. When cooked, sprinkle with chopped parsley and serve.

Boxty

This mainly Ulster dish has made a great comeback in recent years and rightly so. Rosti, which is a similar dish, has been produced in restaurants for years, but traditional boxty with buttermilk is a much more flavoursome Irish version.

MAKES 8

1 kg potatoes

320 ml buttermilk

160 g plain flour

1 tbsp sugar

¼ tsp bread soda

140 g butter

1. Grate the potatoes and place in a clean tea towel. Squeeze all the water out of the potatoes, then place in a large bowl.
2. Immediately pour 270 ml of the buttermilk onto the potato to prevent it from discolouring. Add the flour with the sugar and mix into the potato and buttermilk until you have a thick batter consistency.
3. Dissolve the bread soda in the remaining 50 ml of buttermilk, add to the mix and combine well.
4. Heat a large frying pan and melt 50 g of butter on a medium heat. Add 4 good spoonfuls of the potato mix, leaving some space between them, and cook for 3 minutes on each side or until golden brown. Repeat with another 50 g of butter and the rest of the potato mix.
5. Serve with the remaining butter on top.

Brian's Tip

Serve with grilled bacon and a poached egg for one of the greatest breakfasts ever. Or make a large one the size of a frying pan and top with eggs, tomato and honey.

Potato Farls

This is a great dish for using up leftover mashed potatoes, and it's perfect for breakfast or as a snack or side dish with any main meal.

MAKES 8

75 g plain flour, plus a bit extra for dusting

¼ tsp baking powder

Pinch of nutmeg

Freshly ground black pepper

500 g cooked potatoes, mashed

150 g butter, plus extra for serving

1. Sift the flour with the baking powder and add the nutmeg and some freshly ground black pepper. Add in to your leftover cooked mashed potatoes and stir to combine. It should form a dough.

2. Divide the dough into two halves. Form one piece into a ball, then roll out on a floured surface to create a rough circle about 15 cm in diameter and 5 mm thick. Cut the circle into quarters.

3. Heat a non-stick shallow frying pan over a medium heat with 75 g butter to grease the surface. Transfer the quarters to the pan and cook for about 3 minutes or until golden brown. Flip over and cook the other side for another 3 minutes.

4. Remove to a warm plate, and repeat the process with another 75 g of butter and the other half of the dough mix.

5. Brush with a little more melted butter before serving.

Brian's Tip

Add some cheese and bacon and serve with a poached egg for a quick weekend breakfast.

Breads & Cakes

Scones Three Ways

MAKES 18
BRIAN'S BASIC SCONE RECIPE
225 g self-raising flour
25 g caster sugar

55 g butter, softened
150 ml buttermilk
1 egg, beaten

1. Preheat the oven to 220°C/425°F/Gas Mark 7. Lightly grease a baking sheet.
2. Sieve the flour into a bowl and add the sugar. Rub the butter into the flour, then stir in the buttermilk to form a soft dough.
3. Turn out on to a floured work surface and knead very lightly.
4. Pat out until the mixture is about 2 cm thick. Use a 5 cm cutter to stamp out rounds and place on the greased baking sheet.
5. Brush the tops of the scones with the beaten egg. Bake for 12–15 minutes until well risen and golden.
6. Cool on a wire rack and serve with local butter and good quality jam and cream for a real treat.

IRISH BERRY
Add 50 g each of chopped raspberries and strawberries for an Irish berry scone.
APPLE AND BLUEBERRY
Add 50 g each of peeled, grated apples and chopped blueberries for an autumn treat.
CHEESE AND SCALLION
Add 40 g grated cheese and 2 chopped scallions to the recipe for a savoury scone.

Barmbrack

In Ireland, Barmbrack is a traditionally eaten at Hallowe'en. A coin or a ring is hidden somewhere in the mixture, and whoever finds it will have good luck. It's one of those recipes that tastes better the next day, so I make my barmbrack a day in advance and wrap it in a tea towel overnight.

MAKES ONE 20 cm CAKE

275 g raisins
100 g sultanas
60 g mixed peel
300 ml warm, strong black tea
50 g treacle

2 apples, peeled and grated
200 g dark brown demerara sugar
225 g self-raising flour
¼ teaspoon mixed spice
1 egg

1. Mix the dried fruit, mixed peel, warm tea and treacle in a bowl. Add the grated apples. Cover with cling film and soak overnight.
2. The next day, preheat the oven to 180°C/350°F/Gas Mark 4. Grease and line a 20 cm round cake tin.
3. Add the brown sugar, self-raising flour, mixed spice and egg to the fruit and tea mixture, then stir well until mixed.
4. Pour into the prepared tin and bake for 1½ hours or until it's firm to the touch.
5. Remove from the tin and allow to cool.

Tip

Hide a coin or ring in the centre of the cake prior to baking. Wrap in greaseproof paper before inserting in the mixture.

Bacon and Cheese Soda Bread

I've made this traditional soda bread recipe a bit more exciting with the wonderful flavour combination of bacon and cheese.

MAKES ONE LARGE LOAF

3 rashers dry-cured bacon, finely chopped

225 g self-raising flour

100 g strong cheese, grated

40 g butter

100 ml buttermilk

1. Preheat the oven to 190°C/375°F/Gas Mark 5. Lightly grease a baking tray.
2. Fry the bacon on a dry, hot pan.
3. Sieve the flour into a bowl and add the grated cheese and bacon.
4. Melt the butter and add to the buttermilk. Pour into the flour mix and form a dough by gently mixing.

5. Turn out onto a floured surface and gently shape into a round. Cut a cross on top of the bread and transfer it to the greased baking tray.
6. Bake for 40 minutes.
7. Allow to cool before slicing and serve with real Irish butter.

Tip

Store in an airtight container. For a warm breakfast option, toast a slice and serve with poached eggs.

Thick Batch Loaf

Fresh bread is bread baked that day, and that's the way bread used to be eaten. Quality bread and local butter is seriously good with a cuppa, and many a person's issues have been sorted out over a slice of batch loaf at a kitchen table!

MAKES ONE 900 G LOAF
500 g strong white bread flour
14 g/2 sachets fast-action dried yeast
40 g butter, melted

300 ml lukewarm water
Drizzle of rapeseed oil

1. Put the flour and yeast into a large mixing bowl. Add the melted butter to the water and mix to form a dough.
2. Turn the dough out onto a floured table and knead for 4–5 minutes until smooth.
3. Grease a bowl with the oil, place the dough in the bowl and cover it with cling film. Leave in a warm place until the dough has doubled in size – about 1 hour.
4. Preheat the oven to 190°C/375°F/Gas Mark 5. Grease a 900 g loaf tin.

5. Knock the dough back down and knead to form a loaf shape the size of your tin.
6. Place the dough in the greased tin. Cover with cling film and again leave in a warm place until it has more than doubled in size – about 45 minutes.
7. Bake the bread for 45 minutes. Remove from the tin and allow to cool.
8.Cut in thick slices, lather with butter and serve with a cup of tea.

Tip

Brush the top of the bread with a water and sugar syrup for a rich, dark crust.

Sweet
Treats

Celtic Shortbread Biscuits with Strawberries and Cream

Shortbread with fresh Irish strawberries and cream is as good a treat as you will get anywhere.

MAKES 12

125 g caster sugar
250 g butter, softened
350 g plain flour
100 g semolina

TO SERVE

150 ml fresh cream, whipped
1 punnet of strawberries, sliced
Dusting of icing sugar

1. Preheat the oven to 180°C/350°F/Gas Mark 4. Line a baking tray with parchment paper.
2. Cream 100 g sugar and the butter together in a bowl using an electric mixer. Sieve the flour into the bowl and add the semolina. Using a wooden spoon, fold together to form a dough.
3. Turn the dough out onto a floured surface and knead gently. Then wrap in cling film and place in the fridge for 20 minutes to rest and chill.

4. Roll the dough out to about 75 mm thick Cut into desired shapes (I use a 6 cm round cutter) and place on the lined baking tray. Sprinkle with the remaining 25 g sugar and bake for 15 minutes.
5. Remove from the tray and cool on a wire rack.
6. Serve with whipped cream and sliced strawberries and dust with icing sugar.

Tip

Add a dollop of strawberry jam before the cream for an even fruitier flavour.

Apple and Blackberry Pudding

This pudding is a great supper-time snack or dessert. Apple and Blackberry are very popular Irish fruits, but you can try different combinations with this recipe by including other fruits or adding chocolate chips.

SERVES 12

275 g granulated sugar
275 g butter, softened
2 large cooking apples, peeled and thinly sliced

2 large eggs
Drop of vanilla essence
50 ml milk
450 g self-raising flour, sieved
12 blackberries

1. Add 50 g sugar and 50 g butter to the sliced apples, and then cook gently in a small pot to soften – about 6 minutes. Leave aside to cool.

2. Preheat the oven to 170°C/325°F/Gas Mark 3.

3. In a bowl, beat the remaining 225 g butter with an electric mixer until light and creamy. Add the remaining 225 g sugar and continue to beat.

4. Beat the eggs separately, and then add with the vanilla essence to the mixture. Keep beating until the mixture is light.

5. Beat in the milk and then add the sieved flour. Gently fold the flour in with a spatula, not the electric mixer.

6. Spoon the cooled apples and the blackberries into the mixture and fold gently through – don't incorporate completely – for a marbled effect. Grease 12 individual moulds or ramekins with butter and fill.

7. Bake for 30 minutes. Serve warm with lashings of custard or ice-cream.

Tip

Replace the blackberries with blueberries or strawberries.

Irish Apple Pie

The best way to enjoy a locally grown Irish apple is in a traditional apple pie!

MAKES ONE 20 CM APPLE PIE

250 g plain flour

70 g sugar

125 g butter, softened

2 eggs

4 cooking apples, peeled and sliced

50 g sugar

1 tsp ground cinnamon

Icing sugar to dust

1. Sieve the flour into a bowl, then add the sugar and mix together. Rub in the softened butter until you have a sandy texture. Add 1 whole egg and combine to form a pastry. Knead and shape into a fat disc. Then chill for 20 minutes.

2. Preheat the oven to 170°C/325°F/Gas Mark 3. Grease a 20 cm pie tin or plate.

3. Beat the remaining egg.

4. Roll the pastry out thinly and place on the tin or plate. Add the sliced apples, then sprinkle with cinnamon and sugar.

5. Roll out the pastry lid and use some beaten egg to seal it to the edge of the pastry base. Brush with more beaten egg and bake for 40 minutes.

6. Remove from the oven and sprinkle with icing sugar.

7. Serve with a dollop of freshly whipped cream.

Tip

Add 100 g of blueberries or strawberries for an alternative flavour. Or try baking in a 25 cm square tin and cut into little squares for afternoon tea or supper.

Rhubarb Crumble

Many Irish gardeners grow rhubarb. From a very small plot you can get enough rhubarb to last all year; freeze it, stew it and even make jam with it!

SERVES 4

150 g self-raising flour
50 g light brown sugar
100 g butter, softened
50 g porridge oats

500 g rhubarb, washed and cut into chunks
100 g caster sugar
1 vanilla pod

1. Preheat the oven to 200°C/400°F/Gas Mark 6.
2. For the crumble, mix the flour and brown sugar together and rub in the softened butter until you have a sandy, crumbly texture. Add the porridge oats and gently mix.
3. Spread the crumble out on a tray and bake for 20 minutes until golden brown, stirring halfway through. Set aside to cool.
4. For the rhubarb, simply add it to a pot with the caster sugar and the seeds from the vanilla pod – or use a few drops of good quality vanilla extract.
5. Stew the rhubarb by simmering it for about 15 minutes. Allow to cool slightly.
6. Divide the rhubarb between four 8 cm round dishes. Scatter the crumble on top and place in the oven for 10 minutes. Serve piping hot.

Tip

You have to serve this with custard and ice-cream, mmm ...

INDEX